Patriotic Solos for Melodica

Patriotic Solos for Melodica

10 Patriotic Songs of the U.S.A.

Patriotic Solos for Melodica: 10 Patriotic Songs of the U.S.A.

© 2012 Marco Musica (*www.marcomusica.com*)

ISBN-13:978-1477407677
ISBN-10:1477407677

Contents

Playing guide

Standard notation
Notes are written on a Staff.

Staff
The staff consists of five lines and four spaces, on which notes symbols are placed.

Clef
A clef assigns an individual note to a certain line.
The **Treble Clef** or **G Clef** is used for the Melodica.

This clef indicates the position of the note G which is on the second line from the bottom.

Note
A note is a sign used to represent the relative pitch of a sound. There are seven notes:
A, B, C, D, E, F and G.

Ledger lines
The ledger lines are used to inscribe notes outside the lines and spaces of the staff.

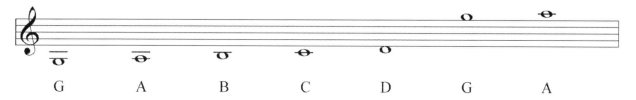

Accidentals
An accidental is a symbol to raise or lower the pitch of a note.

♯ sharp   Next note up half step.

♭ flat   Next note down half step.

♮ natural   Cancels a flat or a sharp.

Note values

A **note value** is used to indicate the duration of a note. A **rest** is an interval of silence, marked by a sign indicating the length of the pause. Each rest corresponds to a particular note value.

o	Whole note	▬	Whole rest
♩	Half note	▬	Half rest
♩	Quarter note	𝄽	Quarter rest
♪	Eighth note	𝄾	Eighth rest
♬	Sixteenth note	𝄿	Sixteenth rest

Dotted note

A dotted note is a note with a small dot written after it. The dot adds half as much again to the basic note's duration.

Tie

A tie is a curved line connecting the heads of two notes of the same pitch, indicating that they are to be played as a single note with a duration equal to the sum of the individual notes' note values.

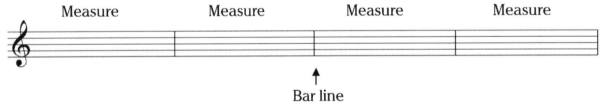

Bars or Measures

The staff is divided into equal segments of time consisting of the same number of beats, called bar or measures.

Measure   Measure   Measure   Measure

↑
Bar line

Time signature

Time signature consists of two numbers, the upper number specifies how many beats (or counts) are in each measure, and the lower number tells us the note value which represents one beat.

one   two   three   four

Example: 4/4 means four quarters, or four beats per measure with a quarter note receiving one beat or count.

Key signature

A Key signature is a group of accidentals, generally written at the beginning of a score immediately after the clef, and shows which notes always get sharps or flats. Accidentals on the lines and spaces in the key signature affect those notes throughout the piece unless there is a natural sign.

Repeat sign

The repeat sign indicates a section should be repeated from the beginning, and then continue on. A corresponding sign facing the other way indicates where the repeat is to begin.

Repeat Sign

First and second endings

The section should be repeated from the beginning, and number brackets above the bars indicate which to played the first time (1), which to play the second time (2).

Fingering

In this book right hand fingering is indicated using numbers above the staff, and left hand fingering is indicated using numbers below the staff.

1 = thumb
2 = index
3 = middle
4 = ring
5 = little finger

Dynamics

Dynamics refers to the volume of the notes.

p   (piano), meaning soft.
mp   (mezzo-piano), meaning "moderately soft".
mf   (mezzo-forte), meaning "moderately loud".
f   (forte), meaning loud.

◁————————————— **Crescendo**. A gradual increase in volume.

▷————————————— **Decrescendo**. A gradual decrease in volume.

Tempo Markings
Tempo is written at the beginning of a piece of music and indicates how slow or fast this piece should be played.

Lento — very slow (40–60 bpm)
Adagio — slow and stately (66–76 bpm)
Andate — at a walking pace (76–108 bpm)
Moderato — moderately (101-110 bpm)
Allegro — fast, quickly and bright (120–139 bpm)
Allegretto — moderately fast (but less so than allegro)
Alla marcia — in the manner of a march
In tempo di valse — in tempo of vals

rallentando — gradual slowing down
a tempo — returns to the base tempo after a *rallentando*

Articulation

Legato. Notes are played smoothly and connected.

Stacatto. Notes are played separated or detached from its neighbours by a silence.

Fermata (pause)
The note is to be prolonged at the pleasure of the performer.

Amazing Grace

Traditional

America (My Country 'Tis of Thee)

Music by Henry Carey

America The Beautiful

Music by Samuel A. Ward

Moderato

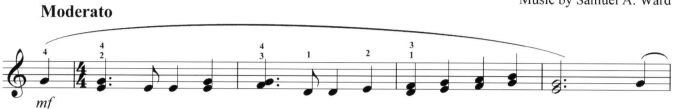

Anchors Aweigh

Music by Charles A. Zimmerman

Alla Marcia

Battle Hymn of the Republic

Traditional

Allegreto

mf

f

rall.

Hail to the Chief

Music by James Sanderson

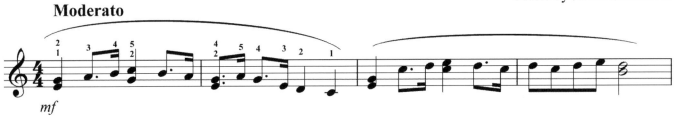

The Star-Spangled Banner

Music by John Stafford Smith

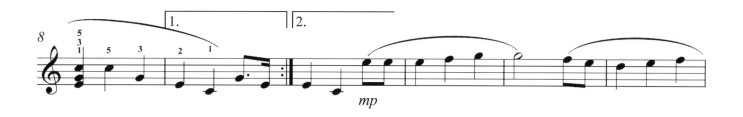

When Johnny Comes Marching Home

Traditional

Yankee Doodle

Traditional

Allegro

You're a Grand Old Flag

Music by George M. Cohan

Alla Marcia

info@marcomusica.com

Made in the USA
San Bernardino, CA
16 June 2017